DOWN TO CLOWN

AN ADULT COLORING BOOK

BY TATIANA GILL

www.tatianagill.com

TEMPLE OF THE
NECRONOMICLOWN SIGIL (2001)

Temple of the Necronomiclown was a group of art clowns who held religious services, went to events and bars around Seattle, and built a temple/bar at Burning Man in 2001. All patrons had to agree to be painted with a clown face to enter the temple and get free cocktails. If a patron arrived naked, they had to agree to wear an adult diaper in order to enter the temple.

PORTRAIT OF SUX DONUT
BLOWING BUBBLES (2007)

Sux Donut was my clown alter ego. I created this drawing to be the homepage for tatianagill.com in 2007. Each bubble linked to a different page.

SAD CLOWN WITH KNIFE (2001)

Originally a small acrylic
painting made for my
brother, Drinkyclown.

Portrait of Firecrotch the Clown (2005)

Firecrotch was a friend and fellow clown.

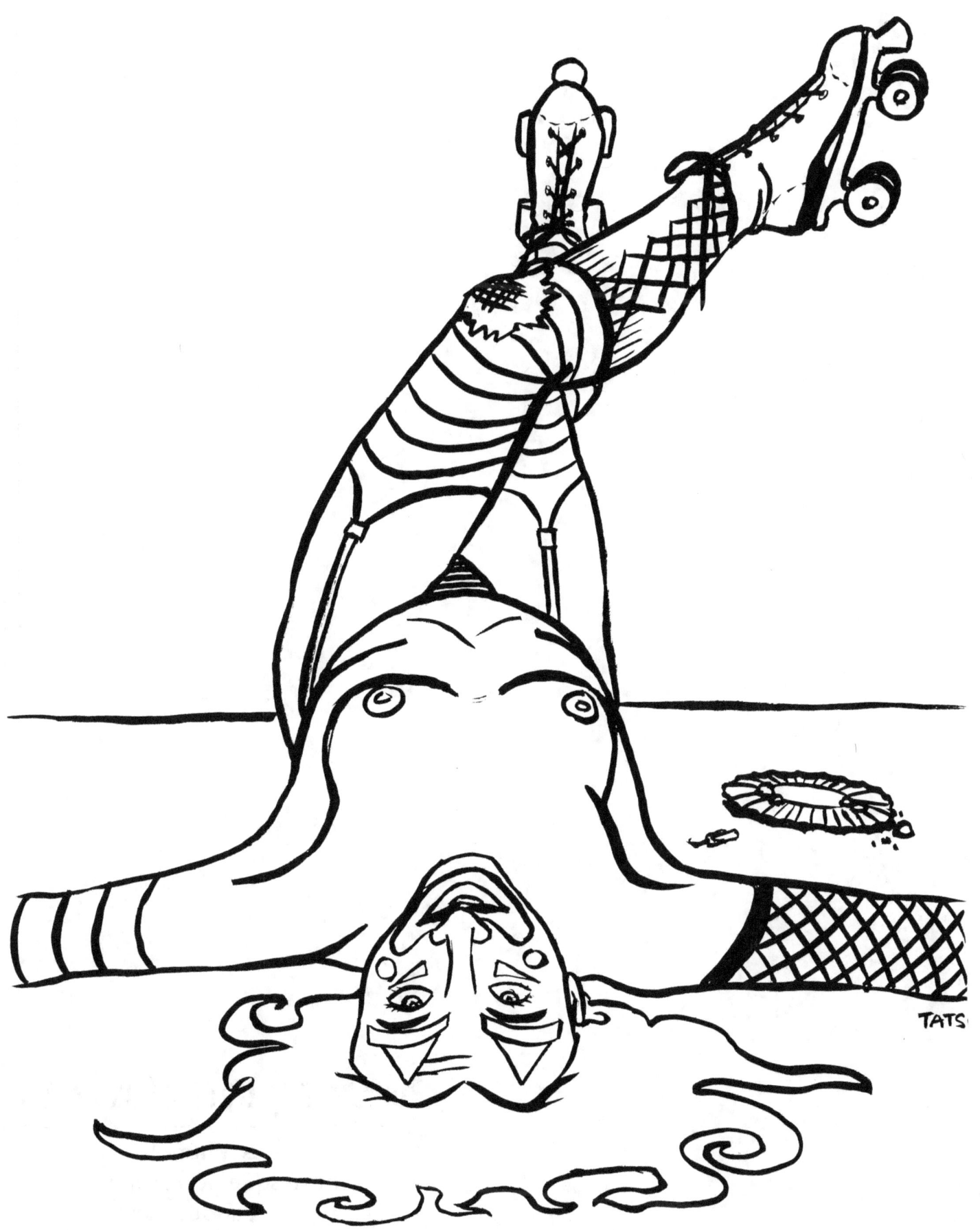

PORTRAIT OF DOTTIE LUX (2005)

Dottie is a famous clown
burlesque performer.
Read all about her at
redhotsburlesque.com.

Portrait of Gagzz the Clown (2005)

Gaggz was a friend, fellow clown, and Floozie's boyfriend.

TATS

PORTRAIT OF SUX DONUT (2005)

As I was eating my first Cupcake Royale cupcake in 2005, I wished that I had a giant version of the cupcake that I could live inside and eat from the inside out.

FRICKER'S FOLLIES
ARTWORK (2001-2008)

The following pages feature the posters I made for Fricker's Follies, along with portraits of all the regular characters. Fricker's Follies was a variety show that (mostly) took place in the Jewelbox Theater inside the Rendezvous Bar, inside the Belltown neighborhood of Seattle, WA. The show ran from 2001-2008. (continued...)

FRICKER'S FOLLIES:
IL DESTINO

...Performances included
comedy sketches, rants,
short films, clowns, dance,
burlesque, sideshow acts,
magicians, music, and more.
(continued...)

LLOYD FRICKER

DRINKY

...The show was hosted by a clown named T.G. Fricker who was supported by a regular cast of characters, threading all the different acts together with an overarching narrative. (continued...)

...In the back of the Jewelbox Theater's green rooms was a back door that led out to Bellotwn's famous "Crack Alley"—and in the Frickers' clown reality it was called "Snap Alley." (continued...)

FLOOZY

BLISTERS

FLUFFY

In Snap Alley, clowns would deal and abuse clown drugs such as Snap, Honk, and Tweet.

Later, Snap Alley would by taken over by tyrants and become a dystopian nightmare. The end.

Sux
Donut

TATS

SHIT
FUCK

Portrait of Floozie the Clown (2005)

Floozie was a friend and fellow performer in Fricker's Follies.

floozie da Clown

TATS

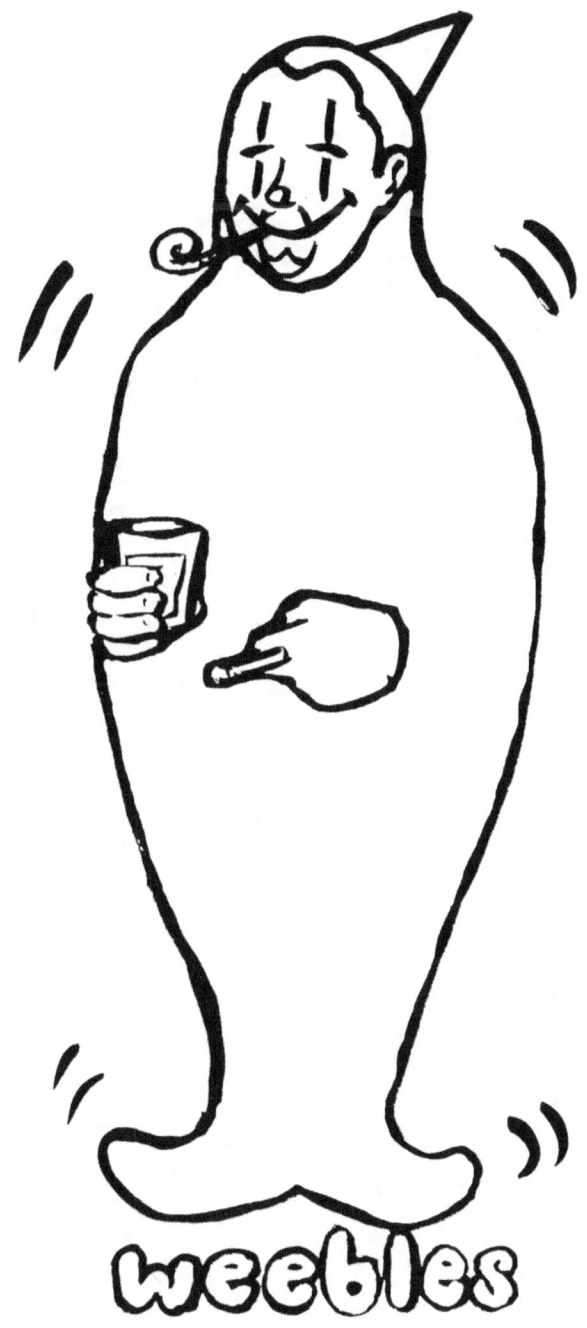

weebles

DR AL ZEUS ISD

FRICKER'S FOLLIES

BEST OF!

THIS EPISODE: BEWARE THE KILL-BOT

don't miss the significant Chicken Cannon!

FEATURING
Baby Gramps
and the girls of
Burning Hearts Burlesque

Rendezvous/ Jewel Box Theater
2320 2nd Ave
& Battery

Sunday February 29

Slobber

PERRY McMENACE

FRICKER'S FOLLIES

DON'T MISS THE CHICKEN CANNON

TATS

EPISODE 8: THE LOST EPISODE!!

TEMPLE OF THE NECRONOMICLOWN

Portrait of Blisters the Clown (2005)

Blisters was a friend and fellow performer in Fricker's Follies.

BURNINGSHAM POSTER (2005)

Burningsham was a huge
warehouse party that
included many clowns.
It was held in the SODO
neighborhood of Seattle the
same weekend as Burning
Man. This image became the
logo for t-shirts, stickers,
and pins declaring "Clowns
Suck."

SKANKSGIVING (2005)

This was also a warehouse party similar to Burningsham, with the distinction that it took place in November and featured mashed potato and gravy wrestling.

FROM THE PEOPLE WHO BROUGHT YOU BURNINGSHAM COMES...

SKANKSGIVING

TATS

WHO WANTS TACOS? (2005)

Portrait of a friend who loved tacos.

Clownicorn (2007)

Sux Donut riding a Unicorn
in Space

BAD VIBES CIRCUS (2005)

The concept of this drawing
was cooked up by Floozie the
Clown, the logo and flag for a
clown-themed art group and
Burning Man Camp.

CONFOUNDED BOOKS
ADVERTISEMENT (2005)

~~~~~~~~~~~~~~~~~~~~~~~~

I drew this as an ad for
the comic and bookstore
Confounded Books, an
amazing small press/zine/
comic bookstore in Seattle
run by an awesome friend.
The ad ran in The Stranger
newspaper.

CONFOUNDED BOOKS

ZINES & BOOKS

ZINES COMIX &

382-3376
315 E PINE

SUX DONUT IN "GIRL CIRCUS" (2002)

Sux Donut had anger management issues. I have taken out the dialogue so you can write your own!

SUX DONUT IN THE ALLEY (2004)

Drawn for the home page of
tatianagill.com.

SUX DONUT IN "PLAYING WITH THE QUEEN OF HEARTS" (2005)

This comic went off the rails and the artist may have been doing rails while she drew it.